GYMNASTICS
THE NEW ERA

Photographs by Mort Engel • Produced by Sydelle Engel

Text by Rosanna Hansen

**Editorial consultant, Robert Hanscom of
Grossfeld's American Gold Elite Training Center**

**Preface by Frank Bare, Executive Director,
United States Gymnastics Federation**

Publishers • GROSSET & DUNLAP • New York
A FILMWAYS COMPANY

To Roni and Andrew, for their patience and understanding.
To C.R.H., for love and forbearance.

CONTENTS

ACKNOWLEDGEMENTS

One of the pleasures in doing this book has been meeting and working with people involved in American gymnastics. Their enthusiasm, cooperation, and advice has been invaluable to us.

We would like to extend our thanks and appreciation to Kurt Thomas, Kathy Johnson, Roger Counsil of Indiana State University, Vanny Edwards of Olympia Manor Training School, Frank Bare, executive director of the U.S. Gymnastics Federation, and the staff and students at Grossfeld's Gymnastics Center.

Also, our thanks to Maureen Broderick and Bernadette LeBlanc, co-coaches of the Signal Hill Elementary School Gymnastic Team, Dix Hills, New York, for all of their assistance with the chapter on beginning exercises. To Beth Broderick, Scott Singhel, and Cynthia DeMaso of the Signal Hill Elementary School Gymnastic Team and to Cara Packard of the Northport School District Gymnastic Program, our appreciation for appearing as models.

A very special thanks to our editor, Nancy Hall, for her unfailing support of this project.

PREFACE

Gymnastics is a sport that has been with us for many years. However, it has only been a prominent sport in the United States for a few years. Names such as Cathy Rigby, Olga Korbut, Nadia Comaneci—and now Marcia Frederick and Kurt Thomas—are well known to the American public. The United States won its first gold medals in a world championship in 1978, and we are looking forward to winning many more.

But it is not just winning medals that is important to gymnasts. Both the experience of being part of a team and working as an individual are the joys of being an athlete.

Gymnasts today are well trained and dedicated, and they spend many hours in preparation for the brief but excellent performances you see on television and in person at gymnastic events.

For any who aspire to participate in amateur sport at its highest and most demanding level, gymnastics awaits you. I hope you enjoy this book and that it contributes to your interest and development as a gymnast or a gymnastics fan.

—Frank L. Bare, Executive Director
United States Gymnastics Federation

UNITED STATES GYMNASTICS FEDERATION

The United States Gymnastics Federation (U.S.G.F.) is the group officially in charge of gymnastics activities in this country. As an official governing body, the U.S.G.F. not only supervises American gymnastics, but it also works to develop the sport at all levels.

Among its many duties, the U.S.G.F. conducts a series of competitions to select the U.S. national gymnastic teams. Internationally, the U.S.G.F. supervises American team participation in such events as the World Championships and the Olympics.

Through its local member organizations, the U.S.G.F. sponsors competitions for boys and girls aged nine and older at the beginner, intermediate, and advanced levels. For those who qualify as international (elite) gymnasts, there is a junior national team program and a national team program. To learn more about U.S.G.F. age-group programs, talk to a local instructor or write to: U.S.G.F., P.O. Box 12713, Tucson, Arizona 85732, (602) 795-2920.

Elena Naimushina of the Soviet Union

GYMNASTICS

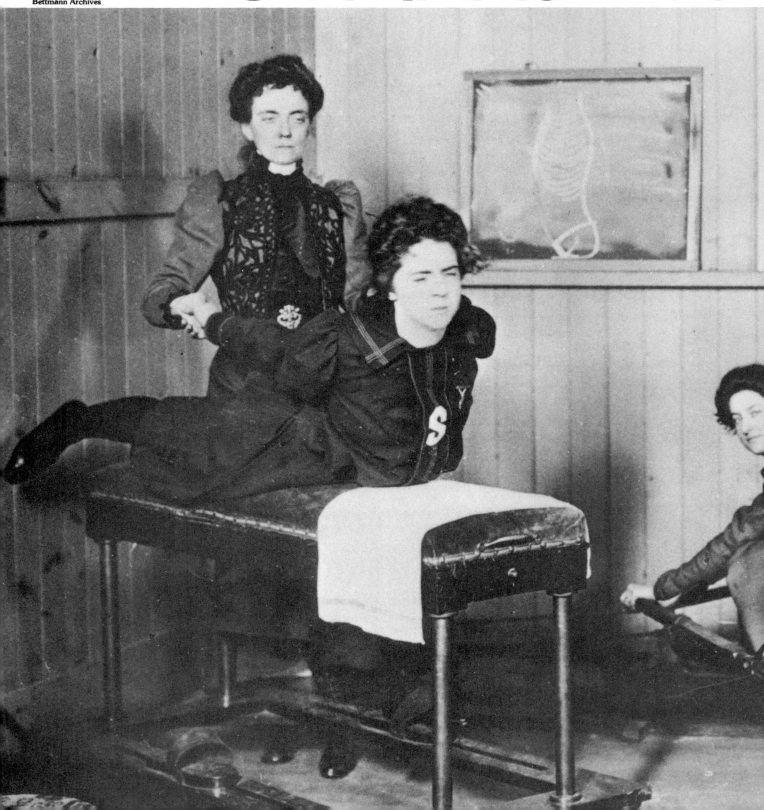

THEN AND NOW

*Ancient Greek vase with a
scene from the Olympics*

HISTORY OF THE SPORT

Did you know that gymnastics is about 5,000 years old? Ancient records show that the early Egyptians practiced their own version of gymnastics 3,000 years before Christ, and China developed its form of the sport about a thousand years later. The Chinese version was called *Cong Fu* and, as you may have guessed, is the ancestor of today's *Kung Fu.*

The Greeks of 2,500 years ago were the first to use gymnastics for sport and personal fitness—earlier, it had been a part of military or personal combat training. In the Greek city of Athens, citizens held gymnastic tournaments, which included tumbling, rope climbing, and similar exercises. The Athenians called their exercises *gymnazein,* which meant "to exercise naked." (They usually performed gymnastics in the nude, and only men participated.) Because they loved athletic tournaments, the Athenians founded the ancient Olympic Games. These competitions were held for more than a thousand years.

When the Romans conquered Greece, they discovered the value of gymnastics for their military training. After the fall of the Roman Empire, however, gymnastics disappeared for centuries.

A woman athlete from an Egyptian tomb drawing

The sport was neglected until the late 1700's, when Frederick Jahn invented new pieces of equipment and started gymnastics clubs *(Turnverein)* in Germany.

His gymnastics societies became quite popular and soon spread to other European countries. In the United States, the first gymnastics club was founded in 1850, and by the 1880's, immigrants from Europe had begun many gymnastics societies in this country.

The first modern Olympic Games were organized in 1896. Appropriately, Athens was chosen as their site, and gymnastics was one of the seven sports included in the competition.

Before the 1970's, however, gymnastics was considered a minor sport in many countries of the world. Outside of the Soviet Union, Japan, East and West Germany, Romania, and a handful of other nations, gymnastics attracted few participants and little public attention. (These countries have traditionally dominated world gymnastics, winning the top awards at world competitions with ease.)

Then, during the 1970's, the world saw an explosion of interest in gymnastics. In the United States, as in many Western countries, gymnastics became one of the fastest growing sports. While there were only 50,000 gymnasts in

When girls studied gymnastics about a century ago, they usually wore full bloomers and blouses with high collars and long sleeves.

Bettmann Archives

Kurt Thomas has led the way in popularizing men's gymnastics.

the entire United States in 1970, that number had grown ten times larger by 1980. Today, more than half a million American gymnasts compete every year.

Gymnastics owes most of its current popularity to two special young women—Olga Korbut and Nadia Comaneci. In the 1972 and the 1976 Olympics, these two athletes won international admiration. Their performances showed over a billion spectators that gymnastics is more than just disciplined exercises—it is a beautiful and exciting art form. Olga and Nadia have inspired thousands of young girls and have done more to popularize women's gymnastics than anyone else in the history of the sport.

Meanwhile, men's gymnastics went largely unnoticed by the public. Yet that began to change in the late 1970's when, for the first time in English-speaking countries, male gymnasts began to attract the recognition they deserved.

Kurt Thomas, generally considered the finest U.S. male gymnast, was the first to gain superstar status, both for his achievements and for his strong audience appeal. Kurt has now become an international favorite.

During the recent surge of interest in gymnastics, the sport itself has changed in many ways. Perhaps the most important change has been the difficulty of skills now performed by gymnasts. In the mid-1970's, Olga, Nadia, and other international competitors started doing very difficult gymnastic skills. Today, women and men gymnasts are able to do tumbling movements that would not have seemed possible only fifteen or twenty years ago!

Take a skill such as a double back somersault (that's two back somersaults in the air before you land), or a double twisting somersault. At one time, few gymnasts in the world could perform these skills; now they are not uncommon. The gymnasts' courage and mastery in performing such hard movements have made today's big competitions especially thrilling to watch.

Meanwhile, the age at which female gymnasts can do such difficult movements has been getting younger steadily. Many top female gymnasts are in their early to middle teens.

Hundreds of thousands of young people are studying gymnastics today, and millions more are avid fans. Through their interest and participation, gymnastics has at last taken its place as a major world sport. A new era has begun.

Bart Conner performs a double back somersault dismount from the parallel bars.

1972: OLGA AT MUNICH

With the help of television, Olga Korbut brought gymnastics to the world's attention at the 1972 Munich Olympics.

At that competition, the petite Soviet gymnast won a silver medal, three gold medals, and millions of devoted fans from around the world. Other women gymnasts had won as many medals, but none had ever captured the audience's hearts as Olga did.

Why did this tiny Russian girl (4 feet 11 inches tall) become the star of the Olympics? The answer lies within Olga herself—in her charm and personality.

When she performed, Olga could express her personality with such joy and emotion that many people found her unforgettable to watch. She brought to gymnastics a new dramatic flair and excitement. As Olga herself once said, "Gymnastics is an expression of my innermost emotions, my response to the love and care with which I have always been surrounded in my life."

International Gymnast

TASS from Sovfoto

1976: NADIA AT MONTREAL

When the 1976 Olympics opened in Montreal, Canada, Nadia Comaneci was completely unknown to most of her audience of millions.

By the end of that opening day, Nadia had scored the first "perfect 10" in Olympic history with a spectacular performance on the uneven bars. No one had thought such a mark was possible!

With that historic performance, Nadia suddenly became the world-wide star of the Olympics. As millions watched in awe, Nadia proceeded to follow her record-breaking routine on the bars with six more performances that earned perfect scores of 10.

The fourteen-year-old Nadia won three gold medals, a silver, a bronze, and also captured the all-around gymnastics title. The first Romanian Olympic champion reigned supreme.

The perfection and difficulty of Nadia's Olympic performances set a new standard in gymnastics and changed the sport forever.

THE CHINESE TEAM

Since gymnastics has emerged as a major world sport, more and more countries are developing teams for international competition. The most exciting new entry in world gymnastics is the People's Republic of China, which has long had excellent national training programs in gymnastics.

The Chinese teams only recently have begun to compete internationally, and they have won medals at most of the meets they have attended. Many experts predict that both the Chinese men's and women's teams will soon dominate the sport.

Besides their tremendous skill as gymnasts, the Chinese team members are known for their open, friendly manner at gymnastic meets. "Friendship first, competition second" is their motto, and their opponents say these fine gymnasts have made those words a reality.

THE

AMERICAN ERA

INTERNATIONAL COMPETITION

A new era in American gymnastics has begun. In the late 1970's, the United States emerged as a real force in world gymnastics competitions. The American breakthrough came in 1978. That year, at the World Games in Strasbourg, France, Marcia Frederick astonished the gymnastics world with her brilliant performance on the uneven parallel bars. Her near-perfect score (9.95 out of 10) earned her the world title in the event—and brought the United States its first world championship ever won by a woman gymnast.

At the same competition in Strasbourg, Kurt Thomas became the first American male in 46 years to win a gold medal in international competition. His performance was one of Kurt's best—a stunning floor exercise that earned him a 9.9 score out of 10. With Kurt leading the way, the American men took fourth place in the team competition. And to make the 1978 World Games a truly banner event for Americans, Kathy Johnson came away with a bronze medal in floor exercise.

The recent American achievements seem even more impressive when one compares gymnastics in the socialist world with that in the free world. Except for Japan and now the U.S., almost all of the top gymnasts in the world have come from a few socialist countries (the Soviet Union, Romania, and East Germany, for example). Why is this the case? In a socialist nation, the government pays for training

In 1978, U.S. gymnasts broke the gold barrier to collect two world championships.

Peter Kormann, who won a bronze medal in floor exercise at the 1976 Olympics, is the first U.S. Olympic medalist in modern gymnastics.

International Gymnast

Before the 1978 World Games, Cathy Rigby's silver medal in 1970 was the best U.S. woman's award in world competition.

amateur athletes. The athletes often go to special government schools that have the most sophisticated equipment and coaching available. Also, they are given privileges that make the decision to go into amateur sports appealing.

In the United States, there is no government support for amateur athletes. (An *amateur athlete* is one who cannot receive payment for performing.) The individual must pay for his or her own athletic training. For many families, the high cost of intensive training is a hardship—or completely impossible.

When one considers what advantages socialist athletes have in training and financial support, the medals being won by American gymnasts today seem truly remarkable.

Since 1978, American competitors have continued to make a strong showing. Kurt Thomas has piled up a long list of international awards, and the excitement doesn't stop with Kurt. Bart Conner, Kathy Johnson, Marcia Frederick, Christa Canary, Donna Turnbow, Rhonda Schwandt, Leslie Russo, Tracee Talavera, and others have brought home important awards and improved the American record at many international meets. And this is just the beginning. U.S. gymnasts are considered a good bet to win more top honors in the future.

In 1979, Tracee Talavera emerged as one of the top gymnasts in the country when she placed third in the American Cup competition. Tracee was 12 years old at the time.

21

A VISIT WITH KURT THOMAS

When the slender young man finished his performance with a dazzling tumbling display, the crowd in Strasbourg, France, went wild. They knew that Kurt Thomas had just won the 1978 world championship in floor exercises—the first time since 1932 that an American had taken a gold medal in men's world gymnastics competition.

Kurt followed up his victory in Strasbourg by sweeping the important American Cup competition in both 1978 and 1979, not only claiming the all-around title, but capturing most of the individual events as well.

With these and many other top awards, Kurt has established himself as one of the finest American gymnasts in history. Also, through his showmanship and audience appeal, he is largely responsible for the new surge of interest in men's gymnastics.

In a recent interview, Kurt told us about himself and some of his experiences in gymnastics. Here's what he had to say:

Q. *How old were you when you started gymnastics? Would you suggest kids begin at that age?*
A. I began gymnastics when I was 14 years old, but it's better to get started when you're younger. If you're younger than 14, it will be easier to develop the strength and flexibility you need for gymnastics.

Whenever you begin, it's important to learn the right way to stretch your muscles and to do each skill correctly. Learning good technique from the very beginning is something I would really emphasize.

Q. *This book is for kids who are interested in gymnastics. What do you think the sport can offer them?*
A. Through gymnastics, you can learn good muscle coordination and develop great control of your mind and body. This kind of control is hard to develop without some sport or physical activity like gymnastics.

Especially if you want to compete, you need to develop good emotional and mental control. It takes work to get yourself confident enough to compete in front of others.

Also, the discipline you learn in gymnastics will help you develop as a person, even if you don't pursue the sport when you get older.

Getting into gymnastics or any activity that keeps your body flexible and conditioned is good for you—and you can really enjoy it!

Q. *What does it take to be a champion?*
A. If you want to be a champion, you have to devote a lot of time and you do have to sacrifice. It's important to set your priorities straight and decide what you want to achieve in gymnastics—then set your mind toward reaching your goal. If you want to be the best, you do have to have dedication.

I find that being a champion requires a lot of time, effort, and patience. My wife tells me all the time that I have patience in just one thing, and that's gymnastics.

On the other hand, if your main goal in gymnastics is to get in shape, or to have fun—that's great, too.

Q. *What kind of sacrifices have you made?*
A. Gymnastics takes most of my time. Because of that, my social life has been somewhat cut off, and it's hard to spend as much time with my wife as I would like.

Q. *Do you have any special foods that you eat?*
A. No, I eat everything I like and I don't have any special foods. I feel very fortunate that I've never had to diet as such. I do cut down my eating a little bit about five days before a meet, but not with any special diet. I just cut down the amounts I eat and make sure I have a well-balanced diet. You do need a balanced diet to keep up your strength.

Q. *How do you feel in a competition when you're competing against your friends or people you know well?*
A. Sometimes it's hard to compete against a good friend. Many times, when I competed, I've been friends with most of the other contestants. That makes it hard, but you have to remember that you want to be the best, and they want to be the best, too. That makes it a good contest, because there's only room for one at the top.

Sydelle Engel with Kurt Thomas at the 1979 U.S. National Championships in Dayton, Ohio.

A VISIT WITH KATHY JOHNSON

Kathy Johnson, U.S. world-class gymnast since 1976, has won many important honors in her sport. These are a few of Kathy's international achievements:

- 1977—American Cup champion
- 1978—Bronze medalist, World Championships, France
- 1978—Bronze medalist, World Cup, Brazil
- 1979—Placed 6th all-around at the World Cup championships in Japan. (Nadia Comaneci placed 4th all-around in that same competition.)

As a member of U.S. international teams for several years, Kathy has seen American gymnastics grow and change. She has some interesting things to say about her sport, which we would like to share with you.

Q. *How did you get interested in gymnastics?*
A. When I watched the 1968 Olympics on TV, I saw the gymnastic events. I liked them so much that I knew right away I wanted to learn the sport.

Before then, I had been doing track and field (sprints and hurdles) when I was in grade school, and I used to do flips and somersaults in my back yard—but I didn't know that what I was doing was called gymnastics.

Q. *When did you actually start?*
A. I was 12 years old when I began studying. That's late for a girl to start gymnastics, but I didn't have an opportunity to begin any sooner.

Q. *Do you have a favorite event when you compete?*
A. I like doing all the women's events, but floor exercise is probably my strongest of the four events. When I perform in floor exercise, I work hard to express myself and give something to the audience. It's a wonderful feeling when the routine goes well and the audience responds.

Q. *What mental attitude should you have to do well in gymnastics?*
A. If you want to succeed in gymnastics, or in any sport, you must have a strong desire to do the very best you can. It's also important to want to win, but I think it's more important to want to do your absolute best.

Q. *Could you tell us some of your personal feelings about gymnastics?*

A. I feel that gymnastics is an art form just as much as it's a sport. To me, performing a routine is like creating a painting or playing beautiful music. A good performance is an artistic expression.

I think gymnastics today needs more stress on its art and beauty. A lot of gymnasts today are concentrating on doing difficult tumbling, and not on creating beautiful movements. Performing difficult skills is important, but I feel that the beauty and elegance of gymnastics is just as important.

Q. *What about nutrition? Do you follow a special diet?*

A. I don't have a special diet, but I think good nutrition is important for every gymnast. I followed a very strict diet for about a year and found that it had a negative effect on my health. I didn't have enough energy for gymnastics, or for anything. So now I am very careful to eat well-balanced meals every day. Sometimes when you are young you worry about looking a certain way, and this is a mistake as far as crash diets are concerned. You don't look good when you don't feel good.

A DAY IN THE LIFE OF AN ELITE GYMNAST

The young men and women you see competing at the Olympics have not become world-class elite gymnasts just by practicing in their back yards or at their local high school gyms. The gymnasts who have qualified as international competitors usually work out for up to six hours a day, five or six days a week. Many of the top American girls actually live at private gymnastic schools, paying thousands of dollars a year in tuition and board.

It takes a great deal of talent, drive, dedication and sacrifice to be an elite gymnast. Gymnastics must be the focus of your daily life. For example, the elite girl gymnasts who live and train at Grossfeld's American Gold Elite Training Center in Milford, Connecticut, follow this daily schedule during the school year:

6 to 8 A.M.   *Wake-up time.* The girls may start the day with an early-morning conditioning workout (for strength and endurance) if their coaches feel they need it. Otherwise, they get up between 7:30 and 8 A.M., have breakfast, and get ready for school.

9 A.M.   *School begins.* By special arrangement, the girls take all their classes in the morning, eat lunch, and leave school by about 1 P.M.

1:30 P.M.   *Training.* By 1:30, they are dressed for practice and are in the gym, ready to start the daily workout. They begin with a dance class and then practice their gymnastics for the rest of the five-hour training period. This training schedule is followed on Monday, Tuesday, Thursday, Friday and Sunday. Although the girls do not work out on Wednesday and Saturday, they are still required to do strength and flexibility conditioning and to jog a couple of miles on these days.

7 to 7:30 P.M.   *Dinner.*

Evening   Two hours for homework. (Most of the girls maintain an "A" average at school.)

10 to 11 P.M.   *Lights out.*

During the year, these girls have one week of vacation and occasional special weekend holidays. Otherwise, their lives revolve around gymnastics.

If you are interested in more information about the elite training programs for girls, here are a few references:

—National Academy of Artistic Gymnastics in Eugene, Oregon. (This is where Tracee Talavera and Leslie Pyfer study.)
—Grossfeld's American Gold Elite Training Center in Milford, Connecticut. (Marcia Frederick and Leslie Russo are two of the top gymnasts at this school.)
—Olympia Manor Training School in Belcher, Louisiana. (Kathy Johnson has trained here.)

Although these schools often have classes for girls as young as three and four years of age, girls do not live in the dormitories until they are about nine, and they often stay throughout their teenage years.

There are also excellent gymnastics clubs where elite girls study during the day but do not live in. Two well-known clubs are:

—Jetes Club in Westminster, California. (Rhonda Schwandt trains here.)
—Parkettes Club in Allentown, Pennsylvania. (Gigi Ambandos is in this club.)

Since boys mature as gymnasts later than girls (most of the important female gymnasts are in their teens), there are no elite live-in schools for young boys. Instead, boys often begin gymnastics in junior high or high school and seek their most intensive training at the college level. However, with increased interest in male gymnastics, many boys are beginning intensive training at earlier ages.

Robert Hanscom, Director, with Muriel Grossfeld at Grossfeld's American Gold Elite Training Center.

EQUIPMENT

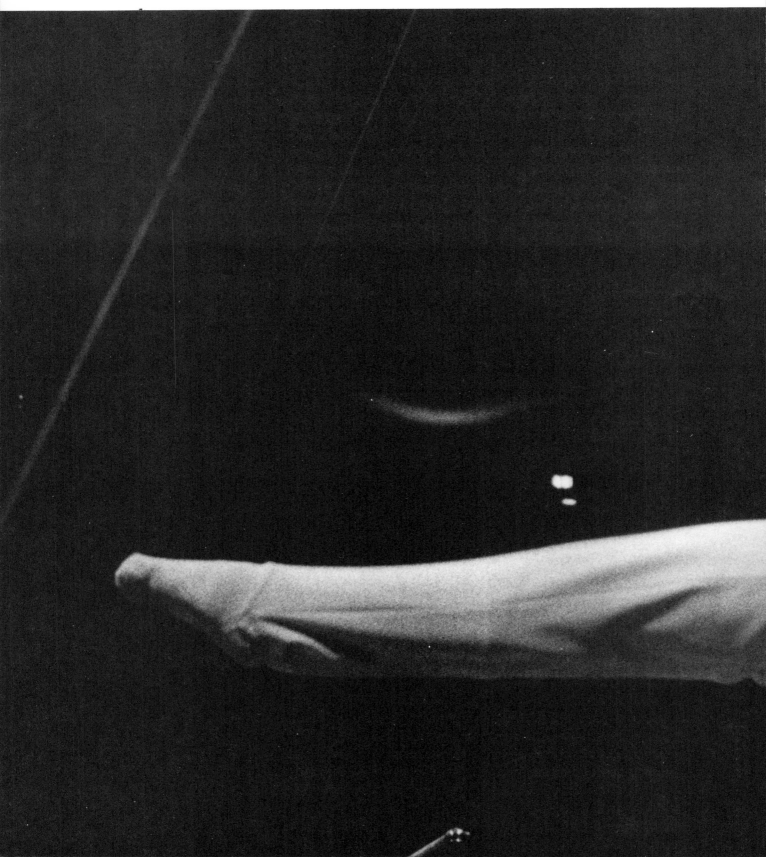

AND EVENTS

Gymnastics is a very honest sport. It admits that men and women have different physical abilities. For example, because of the male bone and muscle structure, men are stronger in their shoulders and arms. Women, on the other hand, are more flexible in their lower torsos and legs.

These different physical abilities are important in gymnastics. As you would expect, in men's gymnastic events, strength moves are stressed, while grace and flexibility are more important for women. (It should be noted, though, that this difference is mainly one of emphasis. To be successful gymnasts, both boys and girls need to work hard to become strong and flexible.)

In a competition, the women gymnasts perform in four events, and the men in six. The women's events are vaulting, uneven parallel bars, balance beam, and floor exercise. For men, the events include floor exercise, pommel horse, still rings, vaulting, parallel bars, and the horizontal bar.

Both men and women perform two exercises or routines for each event. These two kinds of routines are called "compulsories" and "optionals."

Due to differences in bone and muscle structure, male gymnasts like Kurt Thomas can perform movements many women could never do.

The word *compulsory* means something you have to do—that you have no choice. In the *compulsories,* then, each gymnast has to perform the same routine with exactly the same movements. These compulsory routines are assigned in advance so that the gymnasts can practice them.

In the optional routines, the gymnasts are free to choose the movements they like, and to plan their own combination of movements.

This chapter will tell you about each of the 10 basic gymnastic events, looking first at women's gymnastics and then at men's. (Because men and women have similar vaulting and floor exercise events, those events are discussed only in the women's section.)

And many women gymnasts like Leslie Russo do other moves that are beyond a man's ability to flex his body.

VAULTING

Vaulting is one of the oldest gymnastic events. It probably began when Roman soldiers practiced jumping on and off a wooden horse to keep themselves in shape. About a century ago, gymnasts used to vault over a horse that had a fake head and tail, but now the equipment doesn't look like a real horse at all.

To do a vault over the horse, a woman gymnast races forward as fast as possible, takes off from a springboard with a leap, flies through the air until she touches the horse with her hands, propels herself over it, and performs special movements in the air before she lands. All this action takes place in about five seconds!

Before a gymnast begins, she signals to the judges the type of vault she will do. Then, as she performs, she is scored on the correctness of her body position, the height or range of her flight, how well she does her movements, and how securely she lands.

The Tsukahara (pronounced "su-ka-hara") vault requires a cartwheel onto the horse and a one-and-a-half backward somersault before landing. Nelli Kim scored a "perfect 10" on this vault in the 1976 Olympics.

CTK from Eastfoto

Notice how straight the gymnast's body is during this handspring vault. Her body flies high in the air as she leaves the horse.

There are several different types of vaults: (1) straight, (2) handspring, (3) somersault, and (4) twisting vaults. Also, there are some vaults that are combinations of these different types. In each vault, a gymnast's hands must touch the horse during the jump.

Each type of vault is worth a certain number of points, depending on how hard it is to do. For example, one type of handspring vault is worth only 9.20 points, but a more difficult vault called a handspring front somersault vault is rated at a full 10.00 points.

Vaulting for women has become much more difficult and exciting in the last few years. Starting in 1973 and 1974, women began to do dramatic vaults with somersaults that had been done before only by men. Now, many top girl gymnasts can perform vaults rated at the highest difficulty by the time they are eleven or twelve years old.

Men and women gymnasts use the same equipment for vaulting, but women vault across the side of the horse, while men vault down the horse's length, and the horse is set higher for the men.

UNEVEN PARALLEL BARS

The newest and perhaps the most spectacular event for women is the uneven parallel bars. This event was officially introduced at the 1952 Olympic Games. Since then, the bars have rapidly gained in popularity with gymnasts and audiences alike.

Before the uneven bars were developed, women used the same parallel bars as men, but not as successfully. The parallel bars require lots of arm and shoulder strength, which is better suited to men than to women.

The change to uneven bars have made an amazing difference for female gymnasts. On these bars, the women have developed exercises that use swinging and flowing movements instead of arm and shoulder strength.

The higher uneven bar is just over seven-and-one-half feet high, and the low bar is just under five feet. The bars are set about one-and-a-half feet apart, but the distance can be adjusted by as much as 10 inches, depending on the size of each gymnast. If a girl is short, she usually wants the bars set closer together than they are set for a girl who is tall.

After adjusting the bars for her height, a gymnast puts special gymnastic chalk on her hands and thighs to help prevent slipping. Sometimes she chalks the bars, too. She is then ready to begin her exercise.

In a competition, an advanced gymnast would usually start her routine with a mount from a springboard, continue with swinging and circling movements, transfer from bar to bar with turns, jumps, "kips," and other special moves. She would finish with an exciting dismount that may include somersaults or twists, or both.

A routine usually includes from seven to eighteen different moves and may take less than a minute to perform. In her bars exercise, the gymnast is judged on the form of her movements, the different hand grips she uses, the way her body passes between the bars, and the difficulty of her movements. During the routine, she must continue moving the whole time.

Marcia Frederick is famous for her excellent form in the difficult Stalder movement.

Each one of Nadia Comaneci's 1976 Olympic performances on the uneven bars earned her a perfect score of 10.

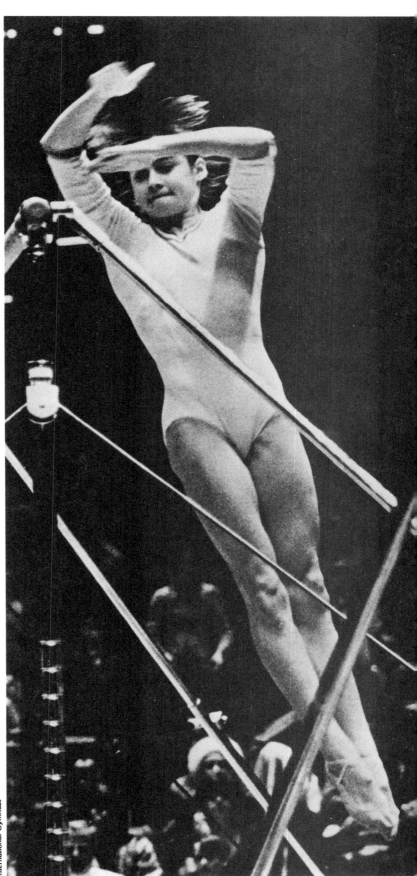

Kathy Johnson chalking the uneven bars before her American Cup performance in 1979.

Elena Naimushina of the Soviet Union circles over the uneven parallel bars in the difficult Comaneci somersault. Her coach stands ready to "spot" or assist her, if necessary.

BALANCE BEAM

A balance beam is just what the name indicates: It's a padded beam on which gymnasts balance and perform a variety of tumbling and dance exercises. The beam stands almost four feet above the ground, is about sixteen feet long, and just under four inches wide. That narrow width is the most crucial four inches in women's gymnastics, since one fall off the beam could certainly cost any performer a win. No wonder many gymnasts say the beam is their biggest challenge!

After a mount from a springboard, the gymnast has between 75 and 90 seconds to do her routine and dismount. Points are taken off her score if she is under or over the time limit, or if she wobbles, stops, or falls. If her routine flows smoothly from one move to the next, she will get additional points.

This event has become increasingly exciting in recent years because the gymnasts are doing more complex skills on the beam. This trend toward difficult beam routines probably began in 1972, when Olga Korbut performed the first back somersault ever done on the balance beam in the Olympics.

Olga's new move caused a huge uproar, because some gymnastic officials were so concerned about the danger of a back somersault on the beam that they tried to ban the move from competition.

The back somersault wasn't banned, however, and the number of difficult moves done on the beam increased rapidly after that. Now many top gymnasts do beam routines that include combinations of back somersaults, aerial walkovers, back handsprings, and other risky tumbling moves.

Back walkover

(Left) Beth Johnson

In her beam routine, a gymnast is required to do jumps and leaps, large and small turns, running and walking steps, and displays of balance.

Tracee Talavera

Nadia Comaneci

(Above) Emilia Eberle of Romania
(Left) Karen Kelsall of Canada

The gymnast's goal is to perform on the beam with the same ease and confidence she would have on the floor.

Grace and poise, shown here by Rhonda Schwandt of the United States, are important qualities for a good balance beam performance.

International Gymnast

Stella Zakharova of the Soviet Union and other gymnasts who perform difficult moves such as this aerial walkover are world-class, elite gymnasts. An average gymnast should never try such dangerous stunts, and should always have spotters beside her when she is on the beam in case she loses her balance.

FLOOR EXERCISE

The floor exercise is supposed to look easy for the gymnast to perform, but the event actually demands every bit of his or her energy and strength. As Cathy Rigby, a former Olympic gymnast, explains: "Performing a good floor exercise is like running a fast 440 in track. It takes all your energy, and loads of endurance."

Endurance means that the gymnasts don't get tired easily. They especially need endurance in floor exercise because they are supposed to do their hardest tumbling moves at the end of their routines, when they're already quite tired.

In the men's floor exercise, the male gymnasts perform exciting tumbling and acrobatic skills without any musical accompaniment. When the men do their best tumbling tricks, such as double front and back flips or twisting somersaults, they are judged on their form and on the height they can reach in the air. If a gymnast doesn't attain enough height during a tumbling move, he may not have enough time to complete all his movements before he hits the ground, and he may not have his feet in the right place for a solid landing.

Male gymnasts, such as Alexander Dityatin of the Soviet Union, must show flexibility, balance, strength, and holding ability in their floor exercise routines.

Kurt Thomas—1978 world champion in floor exercise

Ludmilla Tourischeva of the Soviet Union

The free straddle position requires good balance and strength.

For a good score, a gymnast should show lightness, speed, control, height, and emotional expression in her routine.

Maria Filatova of the Soviet Union

This event is generally considered to be the most beautiful part of women's gymnastics. In her floor exercise, a gymnast combines tumbling, ballet, jazz, modern dance, and other skills into a graceful, flowing routine. The exercises are performed on a mat approximately 40 feet square, within a time limit of one to one-and-a-half minutes. The exercise should cover the whole floor area and include some elements of risk (difficult moves).

Each gymnast performs her routine to music that's chosen to reflect her own personality. The right choice of music is important, so the gymnast can feel its mood and express herself freely. Olga Korbut once refused to do her floor exercises to a piece of music called *Bumble Bee,* because she said her personality wasn't mean and nasty like a bee. Her coaches gave Olga new music that she liked better!

Kathy Johnson

POMMEL HORSE

What's the hardest event in men's gymnastics? Ask any top gymnast that question, and nine out of ten will tell you it's the pommel horse.

Why is this piece of equipment so difficult? After all, the pommel horse isn't as high as the horizontal bar, and it doesn't take the strength needed on the rings.

According to the experts, the pommel horse is considered the hardest event because it demands so many different talents: near-perfect balance, strength, flexibility, graceful movement, and good timing.

During this exercise, the gymnast must include at least three of the popular circle movements known as scissors. These moves are called scissors because the performer splits his legs wide apart to look like an open pair of scissors.

A gymnast will perform a scissors movement by supporting his weight on the handles and swinging his body back and forth above the horse, with his legs split on opposite sides of the equipment. His hips and legs should be lifted as high as possible, legs straight and toes pointed, and his upper leg should be pointed as high as possible toward the ceiling.

In the past, the pommel horse hasn't been a popular event to watch, despite its difficulty. Today, this event is rapidly becoming more popular with both audiences and

In his optional exercise, a gymnast should continually circle the horse with legs held straight and together, and he must travel over the middle and both ends of the equipment (known as the neck, saddle, and the croup). He should not stop at any time or points will be deducted from his score.

The equipment is a vaulting horse with handles (called pommels) added on top of it.

46

gymnasts alike. Kurt Thomas, for example, says that the pommel horse is his favorite event. He feels that the horse exercises are the most "complex and exciting" in men's gymnastics.

One reason the pommel horse has gained in popularity is some exciting new moves that add zip to the routines. Most famous of the new moves is the Thomas Flair, invented by Kurt. The Flair is an amazing series of leg scissors done extremely fast, with great height and flexibility. Brilliant movements like these are making the pommel horse routines fun to watch.

Alexander Dityatin of the Soviet Union, who won the all-around championship at the 1979 World Cup, is considered the world's finest male gymnast.

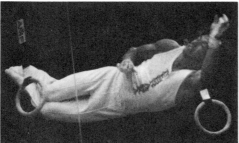

RINGS

The rings require the greatest physical strength of any gymnastic event. Even the names of some ring movements—the "iron cross" or the "dislocate," for example—suggest how hard they must be to perform.

The rings hang almost eight feet in the air, suspended by cables from a high metal frame. If you touch them, they will move back and forth freely. (In your school's gym, the rings may be attached to the ceiling.)

There are two basic kinds of moves on the rings: strength positions and swinging movements. In a strength position, a performer is required to hold his pose long enough to show complete control. (Control means that his muscles shouldn't quiver, and the pose should look easy for him to hold.)

To perform a swinging move correctly, a gymnast has to swing into a position smoothly, without interruption, and then hold the new position. The *dislocate* is one important swinging move. To do it, the gymnast hangs upside down between the rings (an inverted pike position), and then moves his legs up and back while extending his arms to the side. He then "dislocates" his shoulders by turning his thumbs out and makes a complete circle, rotating around the shoulder joint. Despite the sound of the word, in gymnastics, to "dislocate" means only to turn the shoulder joint to its maximum point—never beyond it!

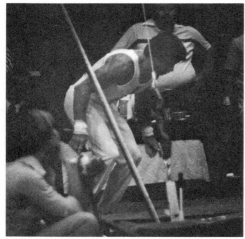

Bart Conner shows good form in his double pike somersault dismount. Note how straight he holds his legs and back.

From half-lever to happy landing

Nikolai Andrianov of the Soviet Union doing a half lever.

Bart Conner performs a handstand, which is a required movement on the rings.

Even though the rings move very easily, a gymnast is supposed to keep them motionless during his routine. Keeping the rings still is what makes this event so difficult. This requires very strong chest and arm muscles.

PARALLEL BARS

Although few spectators would pick the parallel bars as their favorite event, many gymnasts say they like this equipment best of all. One reason they enjoy the parallel bars is that such a wide variety of movements can be performed on the bars.

Also, because the bars can be adjusted in height, the gymnasts can practice new moves with the bars set low. This easy adjustment of height makes the parallel bars an ideal piece of equipment for beginners.

When they compete on the bars, the gymnasts are required to do moves that show both their strength and their ability to balance. They must also do at least one movement of "maximum difficulty." In this type of movement, a gymnast completely lets go of the bars with both hands—and then regrasps both bars at the same time. When the gymnast lets go with both hands at once, you can usually hear a loud gasp from the audience.

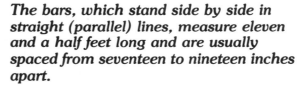

The bars, which stand side by side in straight (parallel) lines, measure eleven and a half feet long and are usually spaced from seventeen to nineteen inches apart.

Kurt Thomas mounts and moves directly into a handstand.

Bart Conner, who won a gold medal at the 1979 World Cup competition in Japan, is one of the best American male gymnasts.

Half lever

Flying backward somersault

Stutz   *Handstand (Right)*

Because most movements on the parallel bars require the gymnast to release at least one of his hands, he needs a fine sense of balance and good timing to perform his routine without wobbles or breaks in his form.

Perhaps the most important move for a gymnast to master on this equipment is the swing into a handstand. When he competes on the parallel bars, a gymnast can hold or "freeze" a position three times, and he will probably do a handstand for one or two of those held movements. In fact, you will rarely see a routine performed without at least one handstand.

The *stutz* is one popular move in which the gymnast has to release his hands. To begin a stutz, he supports himself on the bars with his hands and swings forward. When his legs have swung to their greatest height (about 45 degrees), he will release one hand and start turning his body. When he has twisted far enough, he releases the other hand as well. Then, as his body begins to fall through the air, he will regrasp the bars with both hands. The gymnast can use this move to change his direction on the bars.

In the 1976 Olympics, Mitsuo Tsukahara won the gold medal for the all-around competition and the bronze medal on the parallel bars.

International Gymnast

HORIZONTAL BAR

If you have ever watched a Tarzan movie, you've probably admired the way Tarzan could swing by his arms from a tree branch.

Back in 1812, long before Tarzan movies were made, a man named Friedrich Jahn took the idea of swinging from a tree branch and invented a new piece of gymnastic equipment: the horizontal bar.

Today, the horizontal bar has changed a lot since Jahn first designed it. It now measures eight-and-a-quarter feet long and stands about eight feet high. Because the bar is so high, this event is the most dangerous in men's gymnastics, and is very exciting to watch.

Although Yoichi Tomita is considered one of the finest gymnasts living in the United States, he is not eligible for official U.S. teams because he is not an American citizen.

Ron Gallimore flies over the bar in a straddle vault.

Here, Nikolai Andrianov of the Soviet Union releases one hand from the bar.

A gymnast is required to swing around the horizontal bar without stopping, and should release the bar with one or both hands. The difficult release movements are especially interesting to watch.

The way a gymnast grasps the bar is very important. He will use three main holds: an undergrasp, overgrasp, and cross grasp (one hand over the bar and one hand under). An important "rule of thumb" must be remembered when grasping the bar: *No matter which direction you swing around the bar, your thumbs must point the same way you're moving.* If your thumbs point the wrong way, your hands will peel right off the bar as your body swings, and you'll fall. So, when a gymnast circles the bar with his chest leading, his thumbs must point forward in the direction he's moving (an overgrasp). When he circles backward, his thumbs will point back toward him in an undergrasp.

Eberhard Gienger of West Germany, 1978 world champion on the high bar, is shown here performing a German Giant. Note that his hands are held in an overgrasp.

OTHER FORMS OF GYMNASTICS

So far, all the equipment and events we have discussed belong to the main branch of gymnastics, officially known as Artistic Gymnastics.

There are also several other branches of gymnastics. Two of the more popular of these are modern rhythmic gymnastics and trampoline.

MODERN RHYTHMIC GYMNASTICS

Modern rhythmic gymnastics began early this century in Germany and is rapidly becoming popular in the U.S. and many other countries.

The sport, which is performed only by women, consists of floor exercises done with small hand equipment: balls, hoops, ropes, ribbons, and clubs. The exercises are performed to musical accompaniment.

In a rhythmics competition, the gymnasts perform both as individuals and in teams of six. These exercises are beautiful to watch and are usually popular with audiences.

This branch of gymnastics is currently under consideration as a future Olympic event.

TRAMPOLINE

Back in the Middle Ages, a French acrobat named du Trampoline amazed his audiences with airborne tumbling stunts. Although we don't know much about the type of net or other equipment the Frenchman used, he gave his name to the modern trampoline.

Today, the trampoline is a tightly stretched canvas springboard on which a performer bounces and does a variety of aerial exercises.

Working on the trampoline helps develop balance, rhythm, and timing. These skills are important in any kind of gymnastics. For this reason, the trampoline is often used in training to teach gymnasts difficult tumbling skills.

As a separate branch of gymnastics, trampolining is an official event at a number of competitions and has its own governing organization—the U.S. Trampoline Association. At present, however, trampolining has been eliminated from official college competitions, and its future as a competitive sport is not clear.

SCORING

AND JUDGING

SCORING IN GYMNASTICS

At the 1976 Olympics, Nadia Comaneci astounded an audience of millions when she scored the first "perfect 10" ever awarded in the history of Olympic gymnastics. And that was only the beginning. Before the Olympics were over, Nadia had scored a perfect 10 out of 10 points not once but *seven* times.

Since that historic time in 1976, not only has Nadia continued to receive perfect scores of 10 in additional competitions, but so have quite a number of other female gymnasts.

How do the judges determine that a gymnast has earned a perfect score? And what does "perfect" mean in a gymnastics competition? To answer those questions, let's see how the scoring system works.

INTERNATIONAL SCORING

In an international competition such as the Olympics, each gymnast begins his or her performance with a maximum, or perfect, score of 10. Then as the gymnast performs, points are subtracted from that 10 for each mistake in timing, balance, form, poise, and other factors.

To see how a maximum score of 10 is divided into different sections, look at the point breakdown for women's optional exercises from the international rule book (the Code of Points). The optional exercises are the routines the gymnasts can choose themselves.

Point breakdown for women's optional exercises:		
a. Difficulty	3.00	points
b. Originality and value of connections	1.50	points
c. Composition	0.50	points
d. Execution and amplitude	4.00	points
e. General impression	1.00	points
	10.00	Maximum (perfect) score

As you can see, these different sections add up to a value of 10. To receive a perfect 10, a woman gymnast has to achieve the maximum number of points in each category. (If you would like to know more about any of the terms shown in the chart, check the glossary at the back of this book.)

Whenever a gymnast makes a mistake or fails to do something she should, the judges deduct points from the appropriate category. Besides the deductions illustrated, the judges have a list of every possible kind of error and a point-deduction guide for each one.

In the international men's optional exercises, the point breakdown is somewhat different. In fact, the men have one point category that the women don't have at all. This category is called "risk, originality, and virtuosity" (R.O.V.). Here's what those words mean in gymnastics:

Risk means the gymnast is willing to try something dangerous or difficult and perhaps fail. He doesn't "play it safe."

Originality means the gymnast uses a new movement or a new approach.

Virtuosity means the gymnast performs brilliantly and above the normal technical requirements.

International competitions generally have both optional and compulsory exercises. Although the point breakdown for compulsory routines is quite different (for example, there is no point value allowed for originality), the total still adds up to a maximum score of 10.

Here are some examples of mistakes for which points are deducted:

a. Between $^5/_{10}$ to $^8/_{10}$ of a point would be deducted from this score. Both the rings and his hands are touching, his shoulders are leaning on the straps, and his feet are touching the wires—all deductions.

b. One-half of a point is deducted for this handspring vault. Approximate deductions are: legs apart, $^2/_{10}$; right toe clubbed, $^1/_{10}$; over-arched, $^1/_{10}$; slight bending of elbows, $^2/_{10}$.

c. One-tenth of a point is deducted if a foot is clubbed instead of pointed.

d. One-half of a point is deducted if the gymnast sits down while ending a vault.

In the Olympics and World Championships, the gymnasts are judged in three different competitions: the team competition, the individual all-around competition, and the individual event competition.

In the all-around competition, the gymnasts' scores for each event are added together. The male and female gymnasts who have the highest total or all-around scores win the all-around championships.

THE JUDGES

For both men and women, a panel of four judges scores each performance in a major competition. The four judges independently hand their scores to a head judge. The head judge then disregards the highest and lowest scores, and takes the average of the middle scores. This final number is the gymnast's official score—the one you see flashed on the scoreboard. The use of four judges instead of just one helps to guard against unfair or political judging.

CHANGING THE SYSTEM

Since 1976, with the emergence of so many fine gymnasts who achieve very high scores, the international scoring system has not been completely adequate. This problem is especially true in women's gymnastics.

One change being suggested in women's international scoring would be to give credit for R.O.V. (risk, originality, and virtuosity), as is done in men's gymnastics.

In the United States, this change has already been made. The R.O.V. category was added to the women's national scoring system in 1979 (for optional exercises only). In American women's competitions, the gymnast begins her routine with a maximum score of 9.6. Then, if she includes difficult or original skills in her routine (R.O.V.), the judges can reward her with extra or bonus points. (The maximum or perfect score in this system is greater than 10 points.)

Besides the change in the U.S., other new scoring systems are being tried in Canada and in the Soviet Union. It looks as though a change in international scoring might well be made by or before the 1984 Olympics, but this has not yet been decided.

MAKE YOUR OWN SCORECARD

Here is a sample scorecard you can use to keep a record
while watching the Olympics and other competitions.

WOMEN'S COMPETITION

Name	Team	🪑	⊓⊓	▭	■	AA TOTAL	PLACE

MEN'S COMPETITION

Name	Team	■	🪑	○○	🪑	⊓⊓		AA TOTAL	PLACE

Symbols:

Symbol	Name	Symbol	Name	Symbol	Name
🪑	Horse	■	Floor Exercise	⊓⊓	Parallel Bars
⊓⊓	Uneven Parallel Bars	🪑	Pommel Horse		Horizontal Bar
▭	Balance Beam	○○	Rings	AA	All-around

GETTING

STARTED

GYMNASTICS—IS IT FOR YOU?

Perhaps you've been thinking about taking up gymnastics, but you're not completely sure about it. To help you decide, take a look at some of the benefits this sport can offer you.

• *Superb physical fitness.* Gymnastics is one of the best ways for you to develop a healthy, attractive body. As you practice the sport, you'll improve your coordination, flexibility, balance, and strength. The skills you'll learn are exciting and fun to do and will teach you to use your body with grace and precision.

• *Muscle development.* Girls are often attracted to women's gymnastics because the sport doesn't overdevelop any one group of muscles. A properly trained female gymnast will be very strong, but her muscles will be long and slender, and her body graceful in its movements.

On the other hand, since men's gymnastics stresses strength, boys find that their branch of the sport is great for general fitness and for building strong muscles, especially in the chest, arms, and legs. And in addition to sheer muscle power, the men's sport develops tremendous control, balance, and coordination.

• *Individual growth.* Besides its physical benefits, gymnastics will bring you personal satisfaction as you master

new, exciting skills. And because gymnastics is a highly individual sport, you will learn and develop at your own pace. As you progress, you may or may not choose to perform or compete.

• *Confidence and discipline.* Through studying this sport, you'll gain confidence and self-discipline, and have a chance to show your courage and skills.

• *Sportsmanship.* Roger Counsil, the 1980 U.S. Olympic Men's Gymnastic Coach, emphasizes another personal benefit. In gymnastic classes, students develop an attitude of helpfulness toward their teammates. As they progress, the students learn to assist or "spot" for each other during practice, and they share tips on how to perform new skills. Roger Counsil feels that developing this kind of attitude affects young gymnasts very positively and contributes to their development as people.

Of course, rivalry and intense competition do exist in gymnastics, too, as in any competitive sport. But most coaches agree that in gymnastics, cooperation and competition usually coexist in a healthy way.

• *Fun.* Best of all, most young gymnasts find their sport is exciting to learn—and lots of fun.

HOW TO BEGIN

Here's what it takes to get started in gymnastics: some natural ability, a good program, and a desire to work hard. Let's take a closer look at these things.

First, natural ability. As you know, some people are born with more athletic talent than others, and talent is a factor in gymnastics, as it is in every sport. Now, this certainly doesn't mean that you need a perfect sense of timing or superb coordination, because gymnastics will help you develop these and other physical skills. Also, the amount of talent you were born with won't determine the amount of satisfaction you can get from gymnastics.

On the other hand, natural ability does become important at some levels of *competitive* gymnastics. Talent, although only one of many factors, is essential for gymnasts at the top levels of competition. And, as in every sport, only a select few qualify at the highest levels—not everyone can be an Olympian!

As you progress in gymnastics, you'll learn whether you like it as a hobby, as a physical fitness program, or as a competitive sport. Whatever goals you choose, gymnastics can provide many rewards.

THE RIGHT PROGRAM

How do you go about choosing a gymnastics program? Your first step, of course, is to find out what is available in your area. A large number of local public and private schools now have beginning instruction, as do many other organizations of which you may not be aware.

Here are some of the organizations that provide beginning programs:

—recreational and park departments
—Y.M.C.A.'s (Young Men's Christian Associations)
—Jewish centers (Y.M.H.A.'s and Y.W.H.A.'s)
—American Turners and American Sokols (gymnastic clubs with national programs)
—local independent clubs or private schools for gymnastics.

If you find that several programs are available in your area, here are some tips to help you (and your parents) decide on one:

1) Talk to your physical education teachers. Ask their opinions about each program you're considering.

2) If the program is a member of the United States Gymnastics Federation (U.S.G.F.), ask at what U.S.G.F. levels the gymnasts in that program are competing. Are their gymnasts rated up through the U.S.G.F. intermediate or advanced level? (More information on these levels is available from the U.S.G.F.)

If price, distance, and other factors are equal, a program that goes up through an advanced level is likely to offer you high-quality instruction. Also, the more levels offered by the program, the longer you can continue at the same place as you progress.

3) Next, find out how each program does in competition—including competitions at more than one level of skill. A strong competitive record is one mark of a program's quality, especially if competition is one of your goals.

4) One more tip. After you've picked a program and are ready to enroll, ask if you can sign up for a short period of time (eight weeks, perhaps) to see how well you like it. Many programs offer the chance to enroll on a trial basis when you're new.

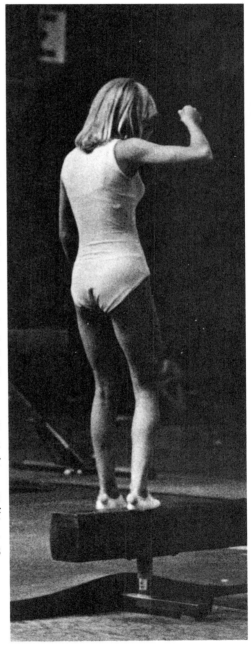

LOOKING GOOD—AND EATING WELL

Looking the part is important in gymnastics. If you want to look your best, check your weight. Is it just right for you, or should you lose a few pounds?

Gymnasts in training know they can't afford to be over-weight for two important reasons. First, excess weight can spoil their body lines and general appearance when they perform. Second, each extra pound they carry costs them that much more energy during practice or competition.

If you eat a healthy, balanced diet every day, you should maintain your correct weight. Be sure you eat proteins, whole grain cereals, milk products, vegetables, and fruits every day. These nutritious foods will give your body the energy and endurance it needs to perform well.

Watching your weight doesn't mean a crash diet, either. Even though you may lose some weight with a quickie crash diet, you will also lose energy and feel cranky. Instead, you should cut out desserts and other sweets, and be careful of starchy foods. If you watch these troublemakers, you'll shed excess pounds in a healthy way. And the energy in your nutritious food will keep the bounce in your gymnastics.

ONCE YOU'VE BEGUN

If you've been studying gymnastics a short time, don't get discouraged if you don't improve as fast as you'd like. Before you can learn many skills, your body needs to build up its fitness. It takes time to develop the strength, flexibility, and endurance necessary to perform gymnastic movements. Those world-class gymnasts you watch on TV have been training for years, and they work long hours every day to perfect their skills. So don't expect too much too soon.

On the other hand, there is something you can do to progress as fast as possible: Exercise on the days you don't have regular gymnastics class. If your schedule is like those in many beginning programs, classes are held two or three times a week, at the most, which is not enough practice to make you a gymnast very fast. When you exercise at home, work on your strength and flexibility exercises, and concentrate on body areas that need improvement.

(One note of caution here: When you work out at home, don't practice the difficult gymnastic skills you're learning in your classes. It's too dangerous for you to try them without trained supervision. Stick to your fitness exercises at home. Remember—you can't improve at all with your arm in a cast.)

The following pages show you examples of good exercises to help develop flexibility and strength.

BEGINNING EXERCISES

WARM-UPS

If you've ever watched a gymnastics meet, you've probably seen the competitors doing preliminary exercises to warm up their muscles and prepare their bodies for strenuous activity.

Warm-ups are important for you, too. Before doing any of the gymnastic exercises in this chapter, you should do at least 10 to 15 minutes of warm-ups. They will get your muscles ready to go, and help prevent any strain or injury.

Before we list sample warm-ups, here are a few tips:

• Do your warm-ups with smooth, continuous movements—no jerking or bouncing up and down: A sudden jerk might tear or strain a muscle.

• Be sure to stretch your chest, shoulders, back, legs, ankles, neck, wrists, and arms.

• Start your warm-up in a standing position. Next, as your muscles loosen, do the exercises on the floor.

STANDING WARM-UPS

Toe Touch

Stand with your feet close together and your arms above your head. Keeping your knees straight, bend forward and touch your toes. Come up slowly until your arms are straight over your head. Then lean back and slowly stretch your upper back.

Side Bends

Stand with your feet far apart and put your hands on your hips. Bend your body sideways, first to the right, then to the left. Next, make a circle by bending to the right, moving your head down in front of your knees, and coming up on the left until you are straight upright again.

Shoulder Swings and Circles

Swing your arms back and forth several times until your shoulders are loosened up. Next, swing one arm in a big circle, and then reverse the circle. Do the same with your other arm, and repeat.

Neck Circles

Put your hands on your hips. Keeping your shoulders level, slowly roll your head in a circle 4 or 5 times. Then reverse direction and do the exercise again.

Foot Flex

Stand with your feet together and slowly rise onto the balls of both feet. Repeat several times; then do the exercise again with turned-out feet (heels together and toes pointed toward the side).

Wrist Flex

Place the palm of your right hand against the fingers of your left hand and gently press the fingers backward. This will stretch your left wrist. Then press your right fingers back with your left palm. Repeat several times.

WARM-UPS ON THE FLOOR

Leg Stretch

Sit on the floor with your legs held together and in front of you. Point your toes. Stretch forward, slowly reaching toward your toes with your hands.

After doing this several times, try it with your feet flexed, and then with your chin up. Keep your knees straight and tight, and try to place your chest on top of your knees as you reach for your toes.

Torso Lift

Lie flat on your stomach with your arms at your side. Slowly arch upward and backward with your head and chest. As you arch, keep your legs straight and your toes on the floor. (Squeezing your legs together will help you keep them straight.)

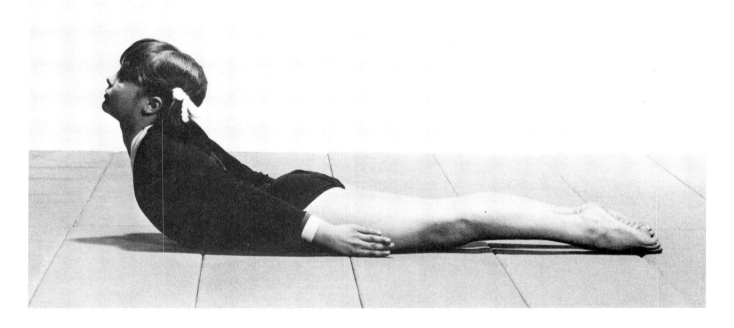

Leg Lift

Lie on your stomach. Slowly lift your legs as high as you can and hold them there for a count of 5.

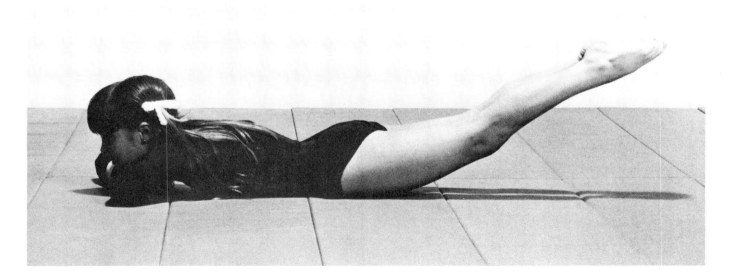

Rocking Horse

Lie on your stomach again. This time, lift your head and chest, arch your back and, at the same time, raise your legs. Grasp your ankles with your hands and gently try to straighten your knees. When you have a good grasp on your ankles, rock back and forth on your stomach.

FLEXIBILITY EXERCISES

You've seen pictures of top gymnasts like Nadia Comaneci and Kurt Thomas bending their bodies into positions that seem almost impossible. For them to do those amazing stunts, their muscles have to be extremely *flexible*.

Flexibility is a key part of gymnastics. Many important gymnastic movements, such as splits and walkovers, require a supple, flexible body.

To help you increase your flexibility, here are a few exercises to stretch and flex your hips, back, legs, and shoulders. Some of them can be done alone and some with a partner.

For each exercise, do the stretching slowly and steadily, and stop if it begins to hurt.

The Split

Everyone knows what the split looks like, but it's important to learn the right way to move your legs into a split position.

Stand in a lunge position. Place your hands on the floor on either side of your front foot. Slowly push backward with your back leg until your front leg is straight. To make it easier, take some of the weight on your hands. You may not achieve a full split at first, but if you keep practicing, you'll be able to do it. Practice the split on both sides for good leg flexibility.

The Bridge

Lie on your back with knees bent and your feet placed close to your backside. Put your palms flat on the floor by your shoulders, with your thumbs close to your ears. Push up until your arms are straight and your body forms a bridge.

From the bridge position, straighten your legs and bring your shoulders over your hands. Doing this exercise will make your spine more flexible.

Hamstring Stretch with Partner

Sit facing your partner with your legs straight and together. Place the soles of your feet against your partner's feet, and stretch your arms out to the side. Lean forward, grasping your partner's right hand, then left hand, then both hands. This exercise will stretch the hamstring muscle in the back of your legs.

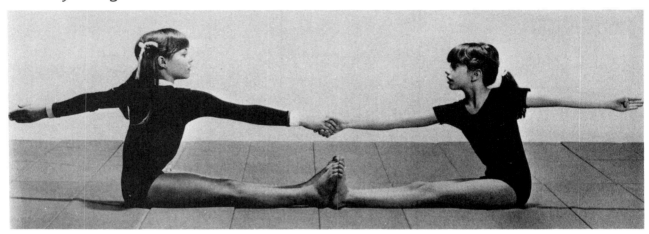

Shoulder Stretch with Partner

Sit with your legs straight and hands at the back of your neck. Your partner will stand behind you with one knee braced between your shoulder blades. To stretch your chest and shoulder muscles, your partner will grasp your elbows and slowly pull them up and back.

Back Stretch with Partner (Row Your Boat)

Sit with your legs apart and your feet against your partner's feet. Holding your partner's hands, bend forward and backward as far as possible. Keep your knees straight, and try to touch the floor both in front and in back.

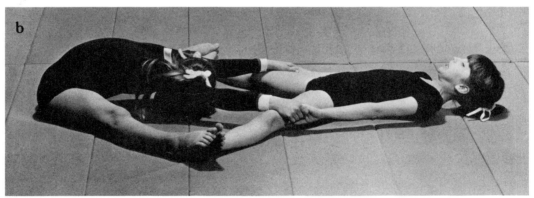

Standing Leg Stretch with Partner

Stand on your left leg with your partner at your right side, holding your right hand with his or her right hand. Your partner will stretch your right leg up and sideways as high as possible. Keep your standing leg straight and your foot on the floor while your leg is raised. If you're having trouble balancing, hold on to the wall or the back of a chair with your left hand. Stop if this starts to hurt.

STRENGTH EXERCISES

Developing strength is an important part of gymnastics for both boys and girls. Girls tend to be weakest in the arms and shoulders, and usually need to work on these areas. Strength in your legs, stomach (abdomen), and other areas will help you develop as a gymnast. These exercises concentrate on building up your muscle strength.

When you begin strength exercises, start by doing each one a few times. As you get stronger, you can build up to 10 or 15 repetitions of each.

Modified Push-ups

Push-ups are great for developing arm strength, but you may find them difficult at first. Start by doing these modified push-ups and work up to a full push-up.

Lie on your stomach with your legs together and place your hands on the floor next to your shoulders. Press with your hands and raise your body while keeping your back straight and your knees and feet on the floor. Push up until your arms are straight. Then lower your body slowly back down to the floor by bending your elbows. Repeat several times.

Push-ups

Lie on the floor as in the modified push-ups. Press with your hands and push your whole body up until your arms are completely straight. Your back and legs should form a straight line. Then lower yourself slowly back to the floor. Repeat three times and build up to ten. (Hint: If you just cannot do a push-up, try lowering yourself very slowly to the floor several times each day. You will find that, in a short time, you will be able to push yourself up.)

a

b

Raised Push-up

If a regular push-up is easy for you, try doing one in a raised position. Start with your legs raised several inches off the floor on a mat or other support. Continue as with a regular push-up.

a

b

One Leg Sit

Stand on one leg with your arms and your other leg raised straight out in front of you. Your free leg should be raised up to the level of your hip.

Squat all the way down on your standing leg, keeping your free leg held straight out in front of you. If you have trouble keeping your balance, hold onto the back of a chair as you learn this exercise.

V-Seat

Lie on the floor with your legs extended straight in front of you. Lift your legs as high as you can and balance on your seat in a **V** position, as shown. Your back and legs should be as straight as possible and your toes pointed. Hold the position for several seconds and repeat. (This will strengthen your hips and stomach muscles.)

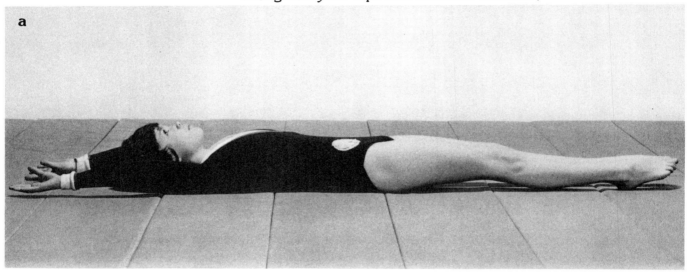

Press

Stand with your legs spread apart (straddle position). Bend over from the waist, placing your palms flat on the floor 6 to 8 inches in front of you. Slowly shift your weight from your feet onto your hands by rolling up on your toes. Let your weight move forward onto your hands until your hips are over your shoulders. This exercise is the first step in learning a press handstand, an important gymnastic move.

a

c

b

Chest Lift with a Partner

Lie face down with your arms stretched over your head. Your partner will hold your feet on the floor. Lift your arms, head, and chest as high off the floor as possible. Hold for 6 to 8 seconds and then slowly lower your body to the floor. Rest and repeat.

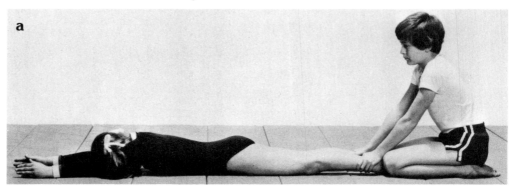

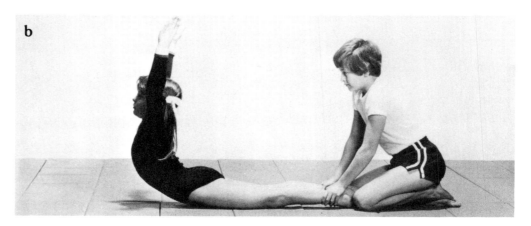

Chest Lift with a Twist

Lift your upper body in the air as you did before, but this time turn to the right side as you lift. After holding this pose for several seconds, return to the floor and relax. Then do it on the left side. (This is good for back and stomach strength.)

Back Lean

Kneel on the floor with arms at your sides. Lean backward as far as you can, keeping your body straight. Return to your starting position and repeat the exercise several times. The back lean will strengthen your back and stomach muscles.

a

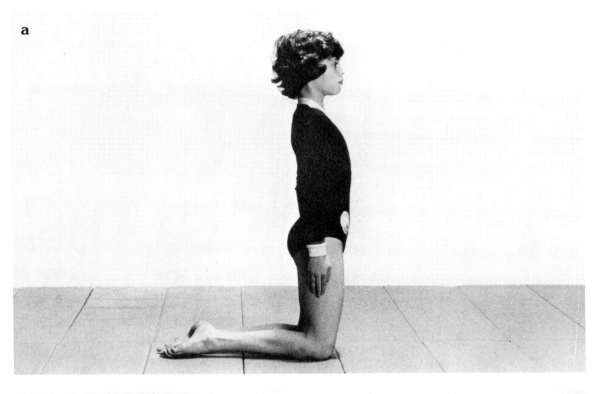

b

DANCE IN GYMNASTICS

Many girl gymnasts study dance as part of their training. Through mastery of dance skills, they learn how to move with precision and grace. Dance movements, such as the ballet poses shown here, are important in floor exercise and balance beam routines.

GLOSSARY

Aerial Walkover   A walkover in which a gymnast rotates through the air without using his or her hands. (See *Walkover.*)

All-around Gymnast   In both men's and women's gymnastics, the competitor who has the highest total score on each piece of equipment.

Amplitude   The greatest possible height and stretching of the body that gymnasts can achieve in their movements.

Artistic Gymnastics   The branch of gymnastics that uses four pieces of equipment for women and six for men. (Other branches of gymnastics include trampoline and modern rhythmic gymnastics.)

Cartwheel   The gymnast turns sideways from a standing position to a handstand, and back to a standing position.

Code of Points   Official international rule book for judging gymnasts. It gives the points deducted for each type of mistake.

Composition   The way the movements of a routine are put together. A good routine will have a variety of movements, speed, and direction.

Compulsories   Assigned routines that must be performed by every gymnast in a competition in exactly the same way.

Conditioning   Exercises and activities that are done to increase strength and endurance.

Difficulty   In a competition, a routine must have a certain number of difficult movements, as listed in the Code of Points. Men have three categories of difficulty (A.B.C. parts) and women have two categories (medium and superior).

Dismount   Final movement of a routine.

Elite Gymnast   A gymnast who is recognized as an international competitor.

Endurance   The ability to exercise hard for an extended period of time without getting tired easily.

Execution   The way a gymnast performs the movements of a routine.

F.I.G.   International Federation of Gymnastics. The world-wide governing organization for the sport.

Flexibility   The ability to stretch the parts of the body with ease in a wide range of motion.

Handspring   A movement in which the gymnast flips from feet to hands and back to feet.

Handstand   A movement in which the gymnast balances with the body held straight above the hands.

Kip   A movement in which the gymnast first *pikes* and then forcefully extends the body outward. Usually performed on the bars. (See *Pike*.)

Movement   One part of an exercise or routine.

Optionals   Routines in which the gymnasts can choose their own movements and combinations of movements.

Originality and Value of Connections.   A scoring category for women's optional exercises. If the gymnast connects her required difficult movements in original and interesting ways, she is given credit in this scoring category.

Pike   A position in which the legs are held straight and the body is bent forward at the hips.

Routine   A planned series of movements performed by the gymnast as a continuous flowing exercise.

Sequence   A group of movements that is part of a gymnast's routine.

Somersault   Any movement in which the gymnast rotates in a complete circle in the air. Also called a somie, or flip.

Spotter   Someone who stands ready to assist a gymnast if she or he needs help.

Spotting   Assisting a gymnast during the performance of a movement. In practice sessions, spotting is done to help a gymnast learn and to avoid possible injury.

Tuck   A position in which the knees are bent, legs are held tightly to the chest, and the body is curled up like a ball.

Tumbling Skills   Tumbling movements, such as rolls, cartwheels, and walkovers, are basic movements learned by gymnasts. Tumbling skills are used in most gymnastic events, and are especially important in floor exercise.

Walkover   A movement in which a gymnast rotates forward from feet to hands and back to feet. (Can also be done backward.)

World Championships   Gymnastic competiton between the countries of the world. (The championships are also called the World Games.)

As this book goes to press, we're pleased to report that the American men have just captured a record-breaking total of eight medals at the December 1979 world gymnastics championships in Fort Worth, Texas.

Kurt Thomas, with five medals to his credit, has surpassed all his earlier records. In the individual finals, Kurt won gold medals in the floor exercise and horizontal bar events, and silver medals in the parallel bars and pommel horse. He also won the silver medal in the all-around, which makes him second only to Alexander Dityatin of the Soviet Union in world gymnastics standings.

Bart Conner, who is now the world's fifth-ranked all-around gymnast, won a gold medal in the parallel bars and a bronze in the vault. As a team, the men brought home the bronze medal—the first team medal ever won by the United States in modern competition.